50 Vegan Cheese Lover's Cookbook Recipes

By: Kelly Johnson

Table of Contents

- Cashew Cream Cheese
- Almond Feta
- Vegan Mozzarella
- Creamy Spinach and Artichoke Dip
- Nutty Parmesan Cheese
- Vegan Ricotta
- Spicy Vegan Queso
- Sun-Dried Tomato and Basil Cheese Spread
- Vegan Blue Cheese Dressing
- Cashew Cheddar
- Vegan Brie with Fig Jam
- Garlic and Herb Cream Cheese
- Smoky Cashew Cheese
- Vegan Pesto Cheese Ball
- Cheesy Broccoli and Rice Casserole
- Vegan Cheddar Cheese Sauce
- Lemon-Dill Vegan Cream Cheese
- Vegan Goat Cheese
- Buffalo Cauliflower Bites with Vegan Ranch
- Vegan Nacho Cheese
- Herb-Crusted Vegan Cheese Wheel
- Vegan Cheddar-Stuffed Jalapeños
- Baked Vegan Mac and Cheese
- Vegan Feta Pasta Salad
- Creamy Vegan Alfredo Sauce
- Spiced Cashew Cheese Spread
- Vegan Creamy Mushroom Soup with Cheese
- Vegan Cheese-Stuffed Shells
- Savory Vegan Cheese Crackers
- Vegan Cheese and Spinach Stuffed Peppers
- Creamy Vegan Caesar Dressing
- Vegan Cheese Fondue
- Vegan Baked Ziti with Cashew Cheese
- Vegan Creamy Tomato Soup with Grilled Cheese
- Vegan Cheese Pizza with Fresh Basil

- Cheesy Vegan Enchiladas
- Vegan Cheesecake with Nut Crust
- Spicy Vegan Cheese Dipping Sauce
- Vegan Cheesy Cauliflower Bites
- Vegan Cheddar and Chive Biscuits
- Vegan Cheese Sliders with BBQ Sauce
- Vegan Jalapeño Popper Dip
- Vegan Cheesy Potato Casserole
- Vegan Lasagna with Cashew Ricotta
- Creamy Vegan Potato Salad
- Vegan Cheese Stuffed Mushrooms
- Vegan Stuffed Acorn Squash with Cheese
- Vegan Cheese and Veggie Platter
- Vegan Creamy Garlic Pasta
- Vegan Cheeseboard with Assorted Nuts and Fruits

Cashew Cream Cheese
Ingredients:

- 1 cup raw cashews, soaked for 4 hours
- 2 tablespoons nutritional yeast
- 1 tablespoon lemon juice
- 1 garlic clove
- Salt to taste

Instructions:

1. Drain and rinse soaked cashews.
2. In a food processor, combine cashews, nutritional yeast, lemon juice, garlic, and salt. Blend until smooth and creamy.
3. Adjust seasoning to taste. Serve chilled.

Almond Feta
Ingredients:

- 1 cup blanched almonds, soaked for 12 hours
- 2 tablespoons lemon juice
- 1 tablespoon apple cider vinegar
- 1 teaspoon dried oregano
- Salt to taste

Instructions:

1. Drain and rinse soaked almonds.
2. In a food processor, combine almonds, lemon juice, apple cider vinegar, oregano, and salt. Blend until a crumbly consistency is achieved.
3. Chill for a couple of hours to firm up before serving.

Vegan Mozzarella

Ingredients:

- 1 cup cashews, soaked for 4 hours
- 1/2 cup water
- 1/4 cup nutritional yeast
- 2 tablespoons tapioca starch
- 1 tablespoon lemon juice
- 1 teaspoon garlic powder

Instructions:

1. Drain and rinse soaked cashews.
2. In a blender, combine cashews, water, nutritional yeast, tapioca starch, lemon juice, and garlic powder. Blend until smooth.
3. Transfer mixture to a saucepan and cook over medium heat, stirring constantly until it thickens. Pour into a mold and refrigerate until firm.

Creamy Spinach and Artichoke Dip
Ingredients:

- 1 cup raw cashews, soaked for 4 hours
- 1/2 cup cooked spinach, chopped
- 1/2 cup canned artichoke hearts, chopped
- 1/4 cup nutritional yeast
- 1 tablespoon lemon juice
- Salt and pepper to taste

Instructions:

1. Drain and rinse soaked cashews.
2. In a food processor, blend cashews, nutritional yeast, lemon juice, salt, and pepper until smooth.
3. Stir in spinach and artichokes. Serve warm with crackers or bread.

Nutty Parmesan Cheese
Ingredients:

- 1 cup raw cashews or almonds
- 1/4 cup nutritional yeast
- 1 teaspoon garlic powder
- Salt to taste

Instructions:

1. In a food processor, combine nuts, nutritional yeast, garlic powder, and salt. Pulse until a fine, crumbly texture is achieved.
2. Store in an airtight container in the refrigerator.

Vegan Ricotta
Ingredients:

- 1 cup raw cashews, soaked for 4 hours
- 1 tablespoon lemon juice
- 1/4 cup nutritional yeast
- 1/2 teaspoon garlic powder
- Salt to taste

Instructions:

1. Drain and rinse soaked cashews.
2. In a food processor, combine cashews, lemon juice, nutritional yeast, garlic powder, and salt. Blend until creamy.
3. Use in pasta dishes or as a spread.

Spicy Vegan Queso
Ingredients:

- 1 cup raw cashews, soaked for 4 hours
- 1/2 cup water
- 1/4 cup nutritional yeast
- 1 tablespoon lime juice
- 1 jalapeño, seeded and chopped
- Salt to taste

Instructions:

1. Drain and rinse soaked cashews.
2. In a blender, combine cashews, water, nutritional yeast, lime juice, jalapeño, and salt. Blend until smooth.
3. Serve warm with tortilla chips.

Sun-Dried Tomato and Basil Cheese Spread
Ingredients:

- 1 cup raw cashews, soaked for 4 hours
- 1/4 cup sun-dried tomatoes, chopped
- 1/4 cup fresh basil, chopped
- 2 tablespoons nutritional yeast
- 1 tablespoon lemon juice
- Salt to taste

Instructions:

1. Drain and rinse soaked cashews.
2. In a food processor, blend cashews, nutritional yeast, lemon juice, and salt until smooth.
3. Fold in sun-dried tomatoes and basil. Serve with bread or crackers.

Vegan Blue Cheese Dressing
Ingredients:

- 1 cup raw cashews, soaked for 4 hours
- 1/4 cup water
- 1 tablespoon apple cider vinegar
- 1 tablespoon nutritional yeast
- 1 teaspoon garlic powder
- Salt and pepper to taste

Instructions:

1. Drain and rinse soaked cashews.
2. In a blender, combine cashews, water, apple cider vinegar, nutritional yeast, garlic powder, salt, and pepper. Blend until smooth.
3. Chill before serving as a dressing or dip.

Cashew Cheddar
Ingredients:

- 1 cup raw cashews, soaked for 4 hours
- 1/4 cup nutritional yeast
- 1 tablespoon lemon juice
- 1 tablespoon apple cider vinegar
- 1 teaspoon smoked paprika
- Salt to taste

Instructions:

1. Drain and rinse soaked cashews.
2. In a food processor, blend cashews, nutritional yeast, lemon juice, apple cider vinegar, smoked paprika, and salt until smooth.
3. Chill before serving as a cheese spread or use in recipes.

Vegan Brie with Fig Jam
Ingredients:

- 1 cup raw cashews, soaked for 4 hours
- 1/4 cup coconut cream
- 1 tablespoon lemon juice
- 1 tablespoon nutritional yeast
- 1/2 teaspoon salt
- 1/4 teaspoon garlic powder
- Fig jam for serving

Instructions:

1. Drain and rinse soaked cashews.
2. In a blender, combine cashews, coconut cream, lemon juice, nutritional yeast, salt, and garlic powder. Blend until smooth and creamy.
3. Transfer to a small bowl or mold and refrigerate for at least 4 hours or until firm.
4. Serve chilled with fig jam on top.

Garlic and Herb Cream Cheese
Ingredients:

- 1 cup raw cashews, soaked for 4 hours
- 1/4 cup water
- 1 tablespoon nutritional yeast
- 2 cloves garlic, minced
- 1 tablespoon fresh chives, chopped
- 1 tablespoon fresh parsley, chopped
- 1 tablespoon lemon juice
- Salt to taste

Instructions:

1. Drain and rinse soaked cashews.
2. In a food processor, blend cashews, water, nutritional yeast, garlic, lemon juice, and salt until smooth.
3. Stir in chopped chives and parsley. Serve with crackers or as a spread.

Smoky Cashew Cheese
Ingredients:

- 1 cup raw cashews, soaked for 4 hours
- 1/4 cup water
- 1 tablespoon lemon juice
- 1 tablespoon nutritional yeast
- 1 teaspoon smoked paprika
- 1/2 teaspoon garlic powder
- Salt to taste

Instructions:

1. Drain and rinse soaked cashews.
2. In a blender, combine cashews, water, lemon juice, nutritional yeast, smoked paprika, garlic powder, and salt. Blend until smooth.
3. Chill before serving as a dip or spread.

Vegan Pesto Cheese Ball
Ingredients:

- 1 cup raw cashews, soaked for 4 hours
- 1/2 cup fresh basil leaves
- 2 tablespoons nutritional yeast
- 1 tablespoon lemon juice
- 1 garlic clove
- Salt to taste
- Chopped walnuts for coating (optional)

Instructions:

1. Drain and rinse soaked cashews.
2. In a food processor, blend cashews, basil, nutritional yeast, lemon juice, garlic, and salt until creamy.
3. Shape the mixture into a ball and roll in chopped walnuts if desired.
4. Refrigerate for 1 hour before serving with crackers or veggies.

Cheesy Broccoli and Rice Casserole
Ingredients:

- 1 cup uncooked rice
- 2 cups broccoli florets
- 1 cup raw cashews, soaked for 4 hours
- 1/4 cup nutritional yeast
- 1 tablespoon lemon juice
- 1 teaspoon garlic powder
- 1/2 teaspoon onion powder
- Salt and pepper to taste
- 1 cup vegetable broth

Instructions:

1. Preheat oven to 350°F (175°C).
2. Cook rice according to package instructions. Steam broccoli until tender.
3. Drain and rinse soaked cashews. Blend cashews, nutritional yeast, lemon juice, garlic powder, onion powder, salt, and pepper with vegetable broth until smooth.
4. In a large bowl, combine cooked rice, broccoli, and cashew cheese mixture. Transfer to a baking dish and bake for 25-30 minutes. Serve warm.

Vegan Cheddar Cheese Sauce
Ingredients:

- 1 cup raw cashews, soaked for 4 hours
- 1/4 cup nutritional yeast
- 1 cup water
- 1 tablespoon lemon juice
- 1 teaspoon turmeric powder
- 1/2 teaspoon garlic powder
- 1/2 teaspoon onion powder
- Salt to taste

Instructions:

1. Drain and rinse soaked cashews.
2. In a blender, combine cashews, nutritional yeast, water, lemon juice, turmeric, garlic powder, onion powder, and salt. Blend until smooth.
3. Pour into a saucepan and cook over medium heat until warmed and thickened. Serve over pasta, veggies, or as a dip.

Lemon-Dill Vegan Cream Cheese
Ingredients:

- 1 cup raw cashews, soaked for 4 hours
- 1/4 cup water
- 2 tablespoons nutritional yeast
- 1 tablespoon lemon juice
- 1 tablespoon fresh dill, chopped
- Salt to taste

Instructions:

1. Drain and rinse soaked cashews.
2. In a food processor, blend cashews, water, nutritional yeast, lemon juice, and salt until smooth.
3. Stir in chopped dill. Serve as a spread on bagels or toast.

Vegan Goat Cheese
Ingredients:

- 1 cup raw cashews, soaked for 4 hours
- 2 tablespoons lemon juice
- 1 tablespoon apple cider vinegar
- 1 teaspoon garlic powder
- 1 teaspoon dried thyme
- Salt to taste

Instructions:

1. Drain and rinse soaked cashews.
2. In a blender, combine cashews, lemon juice, apple cider vinegar, garlic powder, thyme, and salt. Blend until creamy.
3. Shape into a log or ball and refrigerate until firm. Serve with crackers or bread.

Buffalo Cauliflower Bites with Vegan Ranch
Ingredients:

- 1 head cauliflower, cut into florets
- 1 cup all-purpose flour
- 1 cup water
- 1 teaspoon garlic powder
- 1 teaspoon onion powder
- 1 teaspoon smoked paprika
- Salt and pepper to taste
- 1 cup buffalo sauce
- 1/2 cup vegan mayo
- 1 tablespoon apple cider vinegar
- 1 teaspoon dried dill
- 1 teaspoon garlic powder (for ranch)

Instructions:

1. Preheat oven to 450°F (230°C) and line a baking sheet with parchment paper.
2. In a bowl, whisk together flour, water, garlic powder, onion powder, smoked paprika, salt, and pepper until smooth.
3. Dip cauliflower florets into the batter and place on the baking sheet. Bake for 20 minutes, flipping halfway.
4. Toss baked cauliflower in buffalo sauce and return to the oven for an additional 10-15 minutes.
5. For the ranch, mix vegan mayo, apple cider vinegar, dill, and garlic powder in a small bowl. Serve bites with ranch dip.

Vegan Nacho Cheese
Ingredients:

- 1 cup raw cashews, soaked for 4 hours
- 1/4 cup nutritional yeast
- 1/2 cup water
- 2 tablespoons lemon juice
- 1 teaspoon garlic powder
- 1 teaspoon onion powder
- 1/2 teaspoon smoked paprika
- Salt to taste

Instructions:

1. Drain and rinse soaked cashews.
2. Blend cashews, nutritional yeast, water, lemon juice, garlic powder, onion powder, smoked paprika, and salt until smooth.
3. Pour the mixture into a saucepan and heat gently, stirring until warmed. Serve with tortilla chips or veggies.

Herb-Crusted Vegan Cheese Wheel
Ingredients:

- 1 cup raw cashews, soaked for 4 hours
- 1/4 cup coconut cream
- 2 tablespoons nutritional yeast
- 1 tablespoon lemon juice
- 1 tablespoon fresh herbs (thyme, rosemary, or parsley)
- Salt to taste
- 1/2 cup mixed nuts (for crust)

Instructions:
1. Drain and rinse soaked cashews.
2. Blend cashews, coconut cream, nutritional yeast, lemon juice, herbs, and salt until smooth.
3. Shape into a wheel and refrigerate until firm.
4. Crush mixed nuts and coat the cheese wheel in nuts before serving.

Vegan Cheddar-Stuffed Jalapeños
Ingredients:

- 12 fresh jalapeños, halved and seeded
- 1 cup vegan cream cheese
- 1/2 cup shredded vegan cheddar cheese
- 1 teaspoon garlic powder
- 1 teaspoon onion powder
- 1 tablespoon fresh cilantro, chopped

Instructions:

1. Preheat oven to 375°F (190°C) and line a baking sheet with parchment paper.
2. In a bowl, mix vegan cream cheese, vegan cheddar, garlic powder, onion powder, and cilantro until well combined.
3. Stuff jalapeño halves with the mixture and place on the baking sheet.
4. Bake for 20-25 minutes until jalapeños are tender. Serve warm.

Baked Vegan Mac and Cheese

Ingredients:

- 8 oz elbow macaroni
- 1 cup raw cashews, soaked for 4 hours
- 1/4 cup nutritional yeast
- 1 cup water
- 2 tablespoons lemon juice
- 1 teaspoon garlic powder
- 1 teaspoon onion powder
- 1/2 teaspoon turmeric powder
- Salt and pepper to taste
- 1/2 cup breadcrumbs (optional, for topping)

Instructions:

1. Preheat oven to 350°F (175°C).
2. Cook macaroni according to package instructions; drain and set aside.
3. Blend cashews, nutritional yeast, water, lemon juice, garlic powder, onion powder, turmeric, salt, and pepper until smooth.
4. Mix cheese sauce with macaroni and transfer to a baking dish.
5. Top with breadcrumbs if desired and bake for 20 minutes until bubbly.

Vegan Feta Pasta Salad
Ingredients:

- 8 oz pasta of choice
- 1 cup cherry tomatoes, halved
- 1/2 cup kalamata olives, pitted and sliced
- 1/4 cup red onion, diced
- 1/4 cup fresh parsley, chopped
- 1 cup vegan feta cheese
- 2 tablespoons olive oil
- 1 tablespoon red wine vinegar
- Salt and pepper to taste

Instructions:

1. Cook pasta according to package instructions; drain and let cool.
2. In a large bowl, combine cooled pasta, cherry tomatoes, olives, onion, parsley, and vegan feta.
3. Drizzle with olive oil and red wine vinegar, and season with salt and pepper. Toss to combine. Serve chilled or at room temperature.

Creamy Vegan Alfredo Sauce
Ingredients:

- 1 cup raw cashews, soaked for 4 hours
- 1 cup water
- 2 tablespoons nutritional yeast
- 2 tablespoons lemon juice
- 2 cloves garlic
- 1/2 teaspoon salt
- Black pepper to taste

Instructions:

1. Drain and rinse soaked cashews.
2. In a blender, combine cashews, water, nutritional yeast, lemon juice, garlic, salt, and black pepper. Blend until smooth and creamy.
3. Heat the sauce in a saucepan over medium heat and serve over pasta.

Spiced Cashew Cheese Spread

Ingredients:

- 1 cup raw cashews, soaked for 4 hours
- 2 tablespoons nutritional yeast
- 1/4 cup water
- 1 tablespoon lemon juice
- 1 teaspoon smoked paprika
- 1 teaspoon cumin
- Salt to taste

Instructions:

1. Drain and rinse soaked cashews.
2. Blend cashews, nutritional yeast, water, lemon juice, smoked paprika, cumin, and salt until smooth.
3. Chill in the fridge for an hour before serving as a spread with crackers or veggies.

Vegan Creamy Mushroom Soup with Cheese
Ingredients:

- 1 tablespoon olive oil
- 1 onion, diced
- 3 cloves garlic, minced
- 16 oz mushrooms, sliced
- 4 cups vegetable broth
- 1 cup cashew cream (1 cup soaked cashews blended with 1 cup water)
- 1 teaspoon dried thyme
- Salt and pepper to taste
- Fresh parsley for garnish

Instructions:

1. In a large pot, heat olive oil over medium heat. Add the onion and garlic, sautéing until softened.
2. Add the sliced mushrooms and cook until they release their moisture and become golden brown.
3. Pour in the vegetable broth and thyme; simmer for 10-15 minutes.
4. Stir in the cashew cream, blending until smooth. Season with salt and pepper.
5. Garnish with fresh parsley before serving.

Vegan Cheese-Stuffed Shells
Ingredients:

- 12 jumbo pasta shells
- 1 cup vegan ricotta (1 cup soaked cashews blended with 1/4 cup nutritional yeast, 1 tablespoon lemon juice, and salt)
- 1 cup marinara sauce
- 1 teaspoon Italian seasoning
- Fresh basil for garnish

Instructions:

1. Preheat oven to 350°F (175°C). Cook pasta shells according to package instructions; drain and set aside.
2. In a bowl, mix vegan ricotta with Italian seasoning. Stuff each pasta shell with the ricotta mixture.
3. Spread a layer of marinara sauce on the bottom of a baking dish. Arrange stuffed shells on top and cover with remaining marinara.
4. Bake for 25 minutes. Garnish with fresh basil before serving.

Savory Vegan Cheese Crackers
Ingredients:

- 1 cup almond flour
- 1/2 cup nutritional yeast
- 1 teaspoon garlic powder
- 1/2 teaspoon onion powder
- 1/4 teaspoon smoked paprika
- 1/4 teaspoon salt
- 1/4 cup water
- 2 tablespoons olive oil

Instructions:

1. Preheat oven to 350°F (175°C) and line a baking sheet with parchment paper.
2. In a bowl, combine almond flour, nutritional yeast, garlic powder, onion powder, smoked paprika, and salt.
3. Stir in water and olive oil to form a dough. Roll out the dough to about 1/4 inch thick and cut into desired shapes.
4. Place on the baking sheet and bake for 12-15 minutes until golden. Let cool before serving.

Vegan Cheese and Spinach Stuffed Peppers
Ingredients:

- 4 bell peppers, halved and seeded
- 2 cups fresh spinach
- 1 cup vegan cheese (shredded)
- 1/2 cup cooked quinoa
- 1 teaspoon garlic powder
- Salt and pepper to taste

Instructions:

1. Preheat oven to 375°F (190°C).
2. In a skillet, sauté spinach until wilted. Mix with vegan cheese, quinoa, garlic powder, salt, and pepper.
3. Stuff each bell pepper half with the mixture and place in a baking dish.
4. Bake for 25-30 minutes until peppers are tender. Serve warm.

Creamy Vegan Caesar Dressing
Ingredients:

- 1/2 cup raw cashews, soaked for 4 hours
- 1/4 cup water
- 2 tablespoons nutritional yeast
- 2 tablespoons lemon juice
- 1 teaspoon Dijon mustard
- 1 clove garlic
- Salt and pepper to taste

Instructions:

1. Drain and rinse soaked cashews.
2. Blend cashews, water, nutritional yeast, lemon juice, Dijon mustard, garlic, salt, and pepper until smooth.
3. Adjust seasoning if needed. Serve over salad or as a dip.

Vegan Cheese Fondue
Ingredients:

- 1 cup raw cashews, soaked for 4 hours
- 1/2 cup nutritional yeast
- 1/2 cup vegetable broth
- 2 tablespoons lemon juice
- 1 teaspoon garlic powder
- Salt to taste
- Fresh vegetables and bread for dipping

Instructions:

1. Drain and rinse soaked cashews.
2. Blend cashews, nutritional yeast, vegetable broth, lemon juice, garlic powder, and salt until smooth.
3. Heat the mixture in a saucepan, stirring until warm and creamy. Serve with fresh vegetables and bread for dipping.

Vegan Baked Ziti with Cashew Cheese

Ingredients:

- 12 oz ziti pasta
- 2 cups marinara sauce
- 1 cup cashew cheese (1 cup soaked cashews blended with 1/4 cup nutritional yeast, 1 tablespoon lemon juice, and salt)
- 1 teaspoon Italian seasoning
- Fresh basil for garnish

Instructions:

1. Preheat oven to 375°F (190°C). Cook ziti according to package instructions; drain.
2. In a large bowl, mix cooked ziti, marinara sauce, cashew cheese, and Italian seasoning.
3. Transfer to a baking dish and bake for 25-30 minutes. Garnish with fresh basil before serving.

Vegan Creamy Tomato Soup with Grilled Cheese
Ingredients:

- 1 tablespoon olive oil
- 1 onion, diced
- 3 cloves garlic, minced
- 28 oz canned tomatoes
- 2 cups vegetable broth
- 1 cup cashew cream (1 cup soaked cashews blended with 1 cup water)
- Salt and pepper to taste
- Bread slices for grilled cheese
- Vegan cheese slices

Instructions:

1. In a pot, heat olive oil over medium heat. Sauté onion and garlic until soft.
2. Add canned tomatoes and vegetable broth; simmer for 15 minutes.
3. Stir in cashew cream and blend until smooth. Season with salt and pepper.
4. For grilled cheese, make sandwiches with vegan cheese and bread, grilling until golden on both sides. Serve soup with grilled cheese on the side.

Vegan Cheese Pizza with Fresh Basil
Ingredients:

- 1 pizza dough (store-bought or homemade)
- 1 cup vegan mozzarella cheese, shredded
- 1/2 cup marinara sauce
- Fresh basil leaves
- 1 tablespoon olive oil
- Salt and pepper to taste

Instructions:

1. Preheat the oven to 475°F (245°C).
2. Roll out the pizza dough on a floured surface to your desired thickness. Transfer to a pizza stone or baking sheet.
3. Spread marinara sauce evenly over the dough. Sprinkle with vegan mozzarella cheese.
4. Bake for 12-15 minutes or until the crust is golden and the cheese is melted.
5. Remove from the oven, drizzle with olive oil, and top with fresh basil leaves. Slice and serve.

Cheesy Vegan Enchiladas
Ingredients:

- 8 corn tortillas
- 1 cup vegan cheese, shredded
- 1 cup enchilada sauce
- 1 can black beans, drained and rinsed
- 1 cup corn (frozen or canned)
- 1 teaspoon cumin
- Fresh cilantro for garnish

Instructions:

1. Preheat oven to 350°F (175°C).
2. In a bowl, mix black beans, corn, cumin, and half the vegan cheese.
3. Warm tortillas in a skillet until pliable. Fill each tortilla with the bean mixture, roll them up, and place seam-side down in a baking dish.
4. Pour enchilada sauce over the top and sprinkle with remaining vegan cheese.
5. Bake for 20-25 minutes until hot and bubbly. Garnish with fresh cilantro before serving.

Vegan Cheesecake with Nut Crust
Ingredients:

- 1 1/2 cups mixed nuts (walnuts, almonds, or pecans)
- 1/2 cup dates, pitted
- 2 cups cashews, soaked for 4 hours
- 1/2 cup maple syrup
- 1/4 cup coconut oil, melted
- 1/4 cup lemon juice
- 1 teaspoon vanilla extract

Instructions:

1. In a food processor, blend mixed nuts and dates until crumbly. Press the mixture into the bottom of a springform pan to form the crust.
2. Drain and rinse soaked cashews. In a blender, combine cashews, maple syrup, coconut oil, lemon juice, and vanilla extract. Blend until smooth.
3. Pour the cheesecake filling over the crust and smooth the top.
4. Refrigerate for at least 4 hours or until set. Slice and serve chilled.

Spicy Vegan Cheese Dipping Sauce
Ingredients:

- 1 cup raw cashews, soaked for 4 hours
- 1/2 cup nutritional yeast
- 1/2 cup vegetable broth
- 2 tablespoons lemon juice
- 1 teaspoon garlic powder
- 1 teaspoon cayenne pepper (adjust for spice level)
- Salt to taste

Instructions:

1. Drain and rinse soaked cashews.
2. In a blender, combine cashews, nutritional yeast, vegetable broth, lemon juice, garlic powder, cayenne pepper, and salt. Blend until smooth.
3. Pour the mixture into a saucepan and heat over medium heat, stirring until warmed through. Serve with tortilla chips or veggies.

Vegan Cheesy Cauliflower Bites
Ingredients:

- 1 head cauliflower, cut into bite-sized florets
- 1 cup vegan cheese, shredded
- 1/2 cup breadcrumbs
- 1 tablespoon olive oil
- 1 teaspoon garlic powder
- Salt and pepper to taste

Instructions:

1. Preheat oven to 400°F (200°C) and line a baking sheet with parchment paper.
2. In a bowl, toss cauliflower florets with olive oil, garlic powder, salt, and pepper.
3. Spread the cauliflower on the baking sheet and roast for 20 minutes.
4. Remove from the oven, sprinkle with vegan cheese and breadcrumbs, and return to the oven for another 10-15 minutes until golden and crispy. Serve warm.

Vegan Cheddar and Chive Biscuits
Ingredients:

- 2 cups all-purpose flour
- 1 tablespoon baking powder
- 1/2 teaspoon salt
- 1/4 cup vegan butter, cold and cubed
- 1 cup almond milk
- 1 cup vegan cheddar cheese, shredded
- 1/4 cup fresh chives, chopped

Instructions:

1. Preheat oven to 425°F (220°C) and line a baking sheet with parchment paper.
2. In a bowl, mix flour, baking powder, and salt. Cut in vegan butter until the mixture resembles coarse crumbs.
3. Stir in almond milk, vegan cheddar, and chives until just combined.
4. Drop spoonfuls of dough onto the baking sheet and bake for 15-20 minutes until golden. Serve warm.

Vegan Cheese Sliders with BBQ Sauce
Ingredients:

- 12 mini burger buns
- 1 cup vegan cheese, shredded
- 1 cup BBQ sauce
- 1 can black beans, drained and rinsed
- 1/2 cup breadcrumbs
- 1 teaspoon onion powder
- Lettuce and tomato for toppings

Instructions:

1. Preheat oven to 350°F (175°C).
2. In a bowl, mash black beans and mix with breadcrumbs, onion powder, and half the BBQ sauce. Form small patties.
3. Place patties on a baking sheet and bake for 20 minutes.
4. Assemble sliders with a patty, vegan cheese, lettuce, tomato, and a drizzle of BBQ sauce. Serve warm.

Vegan Jalapeño Popper Dip
Ingredients:

- 1 cup raw cashews, soaked for 4 hours
- 1/2 cup nutritional yeast
- 1/4 cup almond milk
- 1 tablespoon lemon juice
- 1 teaspoon garlic powder
- 1 cup diced jalapeños (fresh or pickled)
- 1/2 cup vegan cream cheese
- Tortilla chips for serving

Instructions:

1. Drain and rinse soaked cashews.
2. In a blender, combine cashews, nutritional yeast, almond milk, lemon juice, and garlic powder. Blend until smooth.
3. Mix in diced jalapeños and vegan cream cheese. Transfer to a baking dish.
4. Bake at 350°F (175°C) for 20-25 minutes until hot and bubbly. Serve with tortilla chips.

Vegan Cheesy Potato Casserole
Ingredients:

- 4 cups potatoes, peeled and sliced
- 1 cup cashews, soaked for 4 hours
- 1 cup almond milk
- 1/4 cup nutritional yeast
- 2 tablespoons lemon juice
- 1 teaspoon garlic powder
- Salt and pepper to taste
- 1 cup vegan cheese, shredded
- 1/2 cup breadcrumbs

Instructions:

1. Preheat oven to 350°F (175°C). Grease a baking dish.
2. In a blender, combine soaked cashews, almond milk, nutritional yeast, lemon juice, garlic powder, salt, and pepper. Blend until smooth.
3. Layer half of the potatoes in the baking dish, pour half of the cashew mixture over them, and repeat. Top with vegan cheese and breadcrumbs.
4. Cover with foil and bake for 30 minutes. Remove foil and bake for an additional 15 minutes until golden and bubbly. Serve hot.

Vegan Lasagna with Cashew Ricotta
Ingredients:

- 9 lasagna noodles
- 2 cups marinara sauce
- 1 cup cashews, soaked for 4 hours
- 1/4 cup nutritional yeast
- 1 tablespoon lemon juice
- 1 teaspoon garlic powder
- 1 cup spinach, chopped
- 1 cup vegan mozzarella cheese, shredded

Instructions:

1. Preheat oven to 375°F (190°C). Cook lasagna noodles according to package instructions.
2. In a blender, combine soaked cashews, nutritional yeast, lemon juice, garlic powder, and a pinch of salt. Blend until creamy.
3. In a baking dish, spread a layer of marinara sauce, followed by a layer of noodles, cashew ricotta, spinach, and vegan mozzarella. Repeat layers, finishing with marinara and cheese.
4. Bake for 30-35 minutes until bubbly. Let cool for a few minutes before serving.

Creamy Vegan Potato Salad
Ingredients:

- 4 cups potatoes, cubed
- 1/2 cup vegan mayonnaise
- 2 tablespoons Dijon mustard
- 1 tablespoon apple cider vinegar
- 1 teaspoon garlic powder
- 1/2 teaspoon onion powder
- 1/2 cup celery, diced
- 1/4 cup red onion, diced
- Salt and pepper to taste

Instructions:

1. Boil potatoes in salted water until tender, about 10-15 minutes. Drain and let cool.
2. In a large bowl, whisk together vegan mayonnaise, Dijon mustard, apple cider vinegar, garlic powder, onion powder, salt, and pepper.
3. Add cooled potatoes, celery, and red onion to the bowl and gently mix until well combined. Chill in the refrigerator for at least 30 minutes before serving.

Vegan Cheese Stuffed Mushrooms
Ingredients:

- 12 large mushrooms, stems removed
- 1 cup vegan cream cheese
- 1/4 cup nutritional yeast
- 1/4 cup breadcrumbs
- 1 teaspoon garlic powder
- Salt and pepper to taste
- Fresh parsley for garnish

Instructions:

1. Preheat oven to 375°F (190°C).
2. In a bowl, mix vegan cream cheese, nutritional yeast, breadcrumbs, garlic powder, salt, and pepper until well combined.
3. Stuff each mushroom cap with the cheese mixture and place on a baking sheet.
4. Bake for 20-25 minutes until golden and bubbly. Garnish with fresh parsley before serving.

Vegan Stuffed Acorn Squash with Cheese
Ingredients:

- 2 acorn squashes, halved and seeds removed
- 1 cup quinoa, cooked
- 1 cup vegan cheese, shredded
- 1/2 cup walnuts, chopped
- 1 teaspoon cinnamon
- Salt and pepper to taste
- 1 tablespoon olive oil

Instructions:

1. Preheat oven to 400°F (200°C). Place acorn squash halves cut-side up on a baking sheet. Brush with olive oil and season with salt and pepper.
2. Roast for 25-30 minutes until tender.
3. In a bowl, combine cooked quinoa, vegan cheese, walnuts, cinnamon, salt, and pepper.
4. Fill each squash half with the quinoa mixture and bake for an additional 10-15 minutes until heated through. Serve warm.

Vegan Cheese and Veggie Platter
Ingredients:

- Assorted vegan cheeses (store-bought or homemade)
- Fresh vegetables (carrots, cucumbers, bell peppers, etc.)
- Crackers or bread
- Hummus or guacamole for dipping

Instructions:

1. Arrange vegan cheeses on a serving platter.
2. Cut fresh vegetables into bite-sized pieces and arrange them around the cheese.
3. Add crackers or bread and small bowls of hummus or guacamole for dipping. Serve as an appetizer or snack.

Vegan Creamy Garlic Pasta
Ingredients:

- 8 ounces pasta of choice
- 1 cup cashews, soaked for 4 hours
- 1/2 cup almond milk
- 3 cloves garlic, minced
- 2 tablespoons nutritional yeast
- Salt and pepper to taste
- Fresh parsley for garnish

Instructions:

1. Cook pasta according to package instructions. Drain and set aside.
2. In a blender, combine soaked cashews, almond milk, minced garlic, nutritional yeast, salt, and pepper. Blend until smooth and creamy.
3. In a large skillet, combine cooked pasta and the creamy sauce over medium heat, stirring until well coated and heated through.
4. Garnish with fresh parsley before serving.

Vegan Cheeseboard with Assorted Nuts and Fruits
Ingredients:

- Assorted vegan cheeses (store-bought or homemade)
- Fresh fruits (grapes, apple slices, berries)
- Mixed nuts (almonds, walnuts, cashews)
- Dried fruits (apricots, figs)
- Crackers or bread

Instructions:

1. Arrange vegan cheeses on a large serving board or platter.
2. Fill in spaces with fresh fruits, nuts, and dried fruits.
3. Add crackers or bread for dipping. Serve as a centerpiece for gatherings or as a snack.

www.ingramcontent.com/pod-product-compliance
Lightning Source LLC
LaVergne TN
LVHW081507060526
838201LV00056BA/2975